MACHINES ON THE MOVE

GARBAGE TRUCKS

by Natalie Deniston

TABLE OF CONTENTS

Tadpole Books, an imprint of Jump! Library by FlutterBee

WORDS TO KNOW

can

drives

dumps

grabber

landfill

squish

GARBAGE TRUCKS

It is garbage day.

A garbage truck is big.

It drives.

It has a grabber.

It picks up a can.

It dumps.

Garbage goes in.

Squish!

It makes room for more.

It gets more garbage.

Where does it go?

The landfill!

LET'S REVIEW!

Garbage trucks help keep our neighborhoods clean. What is this truck doing?

INDEX